INTERMISSIONS

Aaron Hundley published his debut novel titled Jack & Evan in May of 2025. He has appeared on KALW's Sights + Sounds and Crosscurrents radio programs. A former college football coach and instructor, he is currently a middle school teacher and resides in Oakland, California with his partner and their two sons.

INTERMISSIONS

Aaron Hundley

Copyright © 2025 by Aaron Hundley
All rights reserved. No part of this book may be reproduced or used in any form without the permission of the copyright holder, except for the use of quotations in a book review.

Second paperback edition December 2025

ISBN 979-8-218-83692-4
www.aaronhundley.com

For my mom Jeanette Ross.
Who always reminded me to focus on one thing at a time.

TABLE OF CONTENTS

INTERMISSION I	01
A DAY IN THE TYPICAL	03
ARE WE THE RIVER OR THE ROCK?	05
SIMILARITIES IN DIFFERENCES	07
FROM DREAM TO DREAM	09
POINT OF DESTINY POINT OF PAST	11
FRIEND OR FOE	13
OPPOSITION	15
INTERMISSION II	17
THOSE BROKE SUMMER DAYS	19
ILLUSIONS OF A NON-ARTIST	21
BIT OF MAGIC	23
THE NEIGHBOR	25
EMPTY CALORIES	27
THE CONCERT	29
THE MAPLE	31
A COURIER	33
INTERMISSION III	35
ACKNOWLEGEMENTS	37

INTERMISSIONS

INTERMISSION I

When the fog holds
the night's stars.
When I stretch my
wings before the Canadians.

It has happened.
Lately it's been during
intermission. When I
empty what has been
collected throughout the day.

Then I hold my hat—
grip the pages and
jot and scribble the
storm of wisdom that
has been carried in.

A DAY IN THE TYPICAL

I have starved from shame.
Over-feasted on euphoria
all within the same hour.

What is a day lived in the typical?
A day of cooked food.
Washed dishes.
A neighborhood walk?

Listening to singing finches.
A day the wind does not beg for
attention— as the face of
the lake shows its youth—
without a wrinkle.

I have seen this day so little.
Though it has been available
to me all my life. Let us
now become more acquainted.

ARE WE THE RIVER OR THE ROCK?

I once heard we must be the river.
Forever giving ourselves to the
changing tides and currents.

I get this.
Yet why do I feel like the rock?
Or more precisely, the tumble stone.
One moment putting up no fight to the will-breaking river,
telling me it's time for change.
While in another, using discernment like a warrior's shield to
defend against the unassuming, yet violent ripples.

It must be how experience schooled me.
Teaching that not all currents come as holy messengers.
That some happen to be imbedded with ungodly intentions.
So in these moments, experience says not to flow.
But ground into the riverbed.
And watch the conniving currents deliver their misleading
whispers—float on by.

SIMILARITIES IN DIFFERENCES

The story is always
of the shy, bullied
and late bloomer.
What of the praised
and highly touted?--

Those who are forced
into the light. It seems
they too should be invited
to the table where compassion
is served.

Here we can learn
of their lives without
complaint or visible
sweat. Of earned trophies
and toil to keep a smile.

Perhaps we can relate
to their scars, from sprouting
in soils, rich with expectations
to achieve.

FROM DREAM TO DREAM

How do we
know that when
our eyes shut,
this too is
not reality–
in a different
realm?

Where lessons
are taught abstractly
on how to clear
debts of the past.
Skills in deciphering
the puzzle may
lessen our blinks
upon waking up.

And forever widen
our eyes to
what is here
and now.

POINT OF DESTINY POINT OF PAST

We do not see the same sun
as it sings and rises in the east.
I have seen mine.

But often I leave for soundless cries
of more familiar warmth.
Yet is this my call to answer?

Or a contract breached?
Signed in the skies with
the dust of stars–

that it is my play in this life
to step outside and to find new
warmth in the cold?

FRIEND OR FOE

As I wander underneath the
protection of massive Monks,
I am the new kid in the quad.
Hardly familiar of the names
and faces I pass.

Within I have become a hybrid
of exhilaration and terror.
With thoughts of which hidden
faces want me dead, and
which is a future friend.

OPPOSITION

Somewhere in the night,
war between world's oldest
rivals rekindled.

It began
how it always has—
heart challenged logic.

Warriors from both sides
squabbled. It is why I
am up before light in a shiver.

Heart kicks to be heard—
in order to take flight
by living out its dreams.

Logic don't like heights.
Who wins?
That depends on the person.

But here I lay with the
audacity of peace.
To prove that there is
logic in following the heart.

INTERMISSION II

D told me
on her return
from "The Boot"
that she had
experienced Siesta.

An eat, sleep,
family break midday.
Oh, my universal
heart wanted more.

Not so of my
American mind.
For Americans work.
Or drown in the
shame of not.

THOSE BROKE SUMMER DAYS

We sipped sugar water
in place of Iced Tea.
Or red Kool-Aid,
instead of Slurpee's.

We ate jelly sandwiches
and cheese sandwiches too.
Cut from a block, the
government issued.

No fine dining, our
Momma would say,
'Go for what you know, y'all,
Tonight I work late.'

Sprints to the kitchen,
roaches occupy a lane,
to reach the lone slice
for the fried bologna
we made.

Dessert was canned fruit,
shielded by bagged peas.
Hope my brother wont find
my stash, eat them and tease.

For a growing child there was little,
for four there was less.
Our bellies were roaring,
but, momma provided her best.

Late hours of tag,
collecting rocks in low tide.
Tuck away into the dusk,
when they seek and we hide.

Reminiscing of those times
and the fuel we lacked, yet
those broke summer days,
I would never give back.

ILLUSIONS OF A NON-ARTIST

One day, as a boy
I opened a big red book.
I think it was red.
I don't remember.

But I am certain it was big.
I skimmed and stopped
at a page that had dates
late February–late March.

My birthday.
Its symbol was two fishies
chasing each other's tails.
"Pisces."

It read:
Imaginative.
Lazy.
Addictive.
Illusions.
Artistic.

It had more. But these
were the words I plucked
from the description—
words that frightened me.

I then told myself I
would not be an artist.
That I am not artistic anyway.

That night, I listened to Stevie.
Bubbled with emotion.
Wrote a poem.
Buried it at the bottom

of the trash to evade
predators — my brothers.

Then went back to
not being an artist.
And now to think
of it. It is possible
the book wasn't big.

BIT OF MAGIC

Years ago, I decided
to scan the tree hours
after present opening.
As it is so with children
I was already
bored with mine.

The skirt was bare,
outside of an
unopened box of
See's chocolate—

but something told
me to reach into
my stocking one
last time.

My little fingers
danced until they
felt something—
making whatever it
was feel alive.

Out came a
green toy frog.
It wasn't there
that morning—
I promise.

My mom wasn't
the type to deny it—
my dad wasn't
the type to do it.

And I understood
by then that
Santa didn't visit
ground level apartments.

So I was left
to believe it
was magic—
I still do.

THE NEIGHBOR

On this wet Christmas day
I noticed our 30-foot neighbor,
now showered and dazzling in
her shimmering golden sweater.

She sneezed off some of
her magical material. Bejeweling
the wagon parked beneath, as she
is the gift that keeps on giving.

EMPTY CALORIES

Hostess cupcakes
were his favorite treat.
Before adulthood his
brown little fingers,
nails jammed with dirt,
would slip a pack of cakes
into his school bag.

Maturity later saved
him trouble–
as he went for
the legal exchange.

He now has given
up the cakes.
Yet he told me saliva
still works his mouth
at the thought–
that magic making bite
when the chocolate
and cream merge.

I asked: why the change?
He said: he had watched
an interview of a famed artist.

The artist was asked
about his shift in style.
And replied, that he was
done chasing the tastiness
of fame– and receiving
no nourishment.

THE CONCERT

The backdrop of the stage
is a bridge. Its peak, fog
frosted. Its base,
reveals its true color.

Not golden like the
headlands it's snugged to.
But a rusty red.

I always stand in the front row.
Can you believe it?

Feeling the power of the
main act breathe in & out.
The mist from her spit, sprinkle
my cheek.

Or hearing a flagpole
riff played by a master. With the legendary
cries of the Gulls as back up.

Oh, and the always inspiring
Pelican dancers, gliding across the
stage in unison.

I get to tell
my son's about this one day.

That their dad lost count of
how many times he has been
able to experience this live concert.

THE MAPLE

They picked up fallen seeds
and released into the air,
to see what helicopters imitate.

The maple above joined the play—
and as if to show how it's done,
mini choppers took flight.

He—as kids do—
opened his hands to chase.
She—as humans do—
had the urge to follow.

Not all are suited for the chase.
So instead she sat—palms up.

It's quite certain he who chased
will one day be rich.

It is too quite
certain that she who sat, already
knows she is.

A COURIER

The wind has messages.
Old memories maybe.
Feel it against your skin.

Or even better,
strip yourself bare —
and it will enter you.

Waiting within is reservations
for four —
frown, smile, weep and laugh.

Welcome their company —
and release once the wind
blows yet again.

INTERMISSION III

If I can't think
in weeks or hours,
I will think in minutes.

If I must, in seconds---

to gift myself the
intermission that
reassembles me whole.

ACKNOWLEDGEMENTS

My deep thanks to Dana for all your love and support. In this case it took form in space, which was needed to write such a book. Thank you to my boys for your warm hugs and kisses on my return home after a writing session.

Thank you to Rebecca Ruger for yet another beautiful book cover. Thank you to P.S. I Love You for publishing some of the poems in this book. Thank you to my big brother Eric for unintentionally confirming that I am not alone in my passion for words.

www.ingramcontent.com/pod-product-compliance
Lightning Source LLC
Chambersburg PA
CBHW020440030426
42337CB00014B/1330